Critical Thinking Skills for Education Students

STUDY SKILLS IN
EDUCATION

Critical Thinking Skills for Education Students

Brenda Judge, Patrick Jones
and Elaine McCreery

First published in 2009 by Learning Matters Ltd.
Reprinted in 2010

British Library Cataloguing in Publication Data
A CIP record for this book is available from the British Library.

ISBN: 978 1 84445 270 5

Cover and text design by Toucan Design
Project Management by Swales & Willis Ltd, Exeter, Devon
Typeset by Kelly Gray
Printed and bound in Great Britain by TJ International Ltd, Padstow, Cornwall

Learning Matters Ltd
33 Southernhay East
Exeter EX1 1NX
Tel: 01392 215560
info@learningmatters.co.uk
www.learningmatters.co.uk

Contents

1. Critical thinking and critical analysis: why are they important?

Introduction

In this chapter you will explore the features of critical thinking and how it contributes to your professional awareness and practice. You will begin to understand that critical thinking is essentially a questioning, challenging approach to knowledge and perceived wisdom. You will understand that critical thinking involves examining ideas and information from an objective position and questioning this information in the light of your own values, attitudes and personal philosophy.

Learning outcomes

Having worked through this chapter you should be better able to understand:

- what critical thinking is;

- why critical thinking is important;

- what the process of critical thinking is;

- how your own values and attitudes impact upon your critical thinking;

- why critical thinking is important to your own professional and personal development.

What is critical thinking?

Critical thinking is essentially a questioning, challenging approach to knowledge and perceived wisdom. It involves examining ideas and information from an objective position and then questioning this information in the light of our own values, attitudes and personal philosophy. It is essential that within the process of critical thinking the writer substantiates the stance they have taken by providing evidence about the issue they are discussing in such a way that their judgements are seen as secure and verified. This chapter explores some of the key principles of critical thinking, to increase your awareness of it and help you to develop analytical and critical skills.

Critical thinking is the ability to think about your own thinking in such a way as to:

- recognise its strengths and weaknesses and, as a result,

- re-present the thinking in an improved form.

To do so you need the ability to be:

- willing to question your views;

- open-minded to the ideas and views of others – just because something is in print, it does not mean it is true;

- able to give your (positive and negative) judgements;

- able to explore the implications of the evidence/literature;

- self-confident enough to explore the evidence presented;

- honest in facing one's own biases/prejudices;

- flexible in considering alternatives and opinions;

- willing to reconsider and revise views where honest reflection suggests that change is warranted.

You also need to be somewhat wary and even sceptical of:

- statements of 'fact' where the point is made obvious and needs no further discussion (i.e. 'It is perfectly obvious that . . .');

- unsubstantiated comments;

- unbalanced arguments;

- bias (whether political, personal or professional);

- anecdotal evidence;

- credibility of sources.

Understanding critical thinking

A great deal of what is taught in a university environment is theory and not fact. Although based on factual evidence, the majority of thinking is conclusions that writers and researchers have drawn from *their* analysis of relevant data. Writers and researchers suggest ideas about what is going on in the world and then research evidence to support or challenge these ideas. In fact, academic debate is founded on an exchange of ideas or theories. If one person puts forward an idea or theory, then other people will often put forward alternatives. When you as a student writer/researcher enter a debate, you become part of this ongoing discussion contributing to the body of knowledge surrounding the issue under discussion.

For example, Piaget and Donaldson's views differ on how children develop. On the one hand, Piaget proposed that children's thinking does not develop entirely smoothly. Instead, there are certain points at which it 'takes off' and moves into completely new areas and capabilities. Piaget saw these transitions as taking place at about 18 months, 7 years and 11 or 12 years. This has been taken to mean that before these ages children are not capable (no matter how bright) of understanding concepts and/or ideas in certain ways. Piaget's proposal has been used as the basis for scheduling the school curriculum. On the other hand, Donaldson's theory focuses on the concept of embedded and disembedded thinking. Thinking that is embedded or placed in a familiar context makes 'human' sense and is more easily understood by children who are able to reason with it. When children are asked to do something outside their limits of human sense – that is, when something is unfamiliar or unrealistic – their thinking is disembedded and it fails to make sense. Donaldson challenged Piaget's theory of children having a ceiling on their thinking. She encouraged practitioners to seek out what children are able to do rather than focusing on the things they cannot do. She believed that in order to educate young children effectively, practitioners must decentre and try to present things from a child's point of view. What this means for you is that, while there is often a dominant prevailing viewpoint on a particular issue, there will be alternative viewpoints that you can explore and analyse through literature. You can always find alternative viewpoints if you look hard enough.

To reiterate, critical thinking is the ability to think about your own thinking in such a way that you recognise its strengths and weaknesses and, as a result, reconsider your viewpoint and reconstruct your thinking in an improved form. To be able to do this it is necessary to be willing to question your own views and be open-minded to the ideas and views of others. You also need to be confident enough to recognise that just because something is in print does not mean it is true.

Why is critical thinking important?

If you are able to challenge others' ideas in this way it enables you to make your own judgements, which in turn improves your self-confidence in exploring any evidence or literature and its implications.

Some of the most important skills you will need to learn as an education student are the ability to think both critically and objectively about an issue and present a well-constructed argument. Critical and analytical thinking skills such as these will be essential to most aspects of your study, whether you are listening to lectures, contributing to seminars or reading about your subject. This chapter mainly focuses on critical analysis for written work as nothing gains or loses marks on assignments more than the quality of the written argument.

Argument here does not mean disagreement; it simply means presenting a strong case to support a point of view. You do not have to be an argumentative person to do this. On the contrary, good critical writing means using reason and evidence to support your point.

However, essential to any analysis is the ability to be honest about your own biases and prejudices, flexible in considering alternatives and opinions, and willing to reconsider and revise views where honest reflection suggests that change is warranted. You also need to cultivate a healthy scepticism of: statements which begin with 'It is obvious that. . .'; arguments which are unsubstantiated and unbalanced; and arguments which have a particular political, professional or anecdotal bias (as opposed to researched evidence). You also need to verify the source of any research/literature you are considering.

Two common problems can lead to confusion when thinking critically about a subject: ambiguity and subjectivity.

Ambiguity

A word is ambiguous if it has several different meanings.

'Partnership', for example, might specifically refer to a legally binding collaboration between two or more people. More generally, it may mean co-operation between interested stakeholders in a particular project. In education it can be interpreted as regarding parents as co-educators of their children. In a broader sense it can be understood as a partnership between investors in the education system, such as national government, local government and perhaps even business. So collaboration can be a partnership in one of these senses but not in another. Consulting with parents at parent evenings and providing information to those parents could be seen by some as a partnership and by others as paying lip service to that partnership. The word 'partnership' on its own could refer to any of these types of partnerships. Therefore, unless the context makes it clear which meaning is intended, it is sometimes difficult to distinguish between them.

Subjectivity

Problems of subjectivity arise when, even once all ambiguity has been removed from a term, people still disagree about its meaning.

The concept of a partnership with parents, for example, is a very subjective one. Two people may agree precisely about what that partnership is (e.g. they may agree that it is dialogue between teachers and parents), but disagree about the depth of involvement both parties should have. The depth of the involvement will be influenced by personal philosophy and values. For example, one person may see parents as the initial educators of their children and people who have a legitimate stakehold in their children's future, whereas another person may disagree, believing the 'professionals' are the people with the information which has to be shared with the other interested partners. These examples show that even when a concept is clearly understood and agreed by all parties, there are differences in the application of the concept due to its subjective nature.

At the heart of critical thinking (and, indeed, critical reading and writing) is the notion of 'objectivity'. Being objective means that you read, write and think without bias, take into account all the facts and possible explanations and draw on available evidence. Expressing personal opinions, on the other hand, is a subjective endeavour. However, personal opinions can become more objective if you subject them to rigorous questioning.

Practical task

During a seminar James suggested that some parents, especially those from deprived backgrounds, have little understanding of the needs of their children and are unable to make appropriate judgements. Megan asked him on what evidence he was basing this statement. James realised that what he had said was very subjective.

Try to reword James's statement to make it less subjective.

One possible version is:

Class differences in educational achievement have persisted since the 1950s. J.W.B. Douglas (1964) argued that the key to higher achievement was parental interest and that middle-class parents were more interested in education than their working-class peers. However, Blackstone and Mortimer in 1994 argued that, because of their own experiences, working-class parents did not feel as confident about dealing with schools as their middle-class peers.

Reflective task

For the above practical task:

- Make a list of the words you removed or changed to make the statement less subjective.

- What type of words were these?

Practical task

Subjectivity and objectivity

a)

- Select a copy of a professional journal or newspaper.

- Read the editorial or readers' comments section.

- Try to identify the words that make the section emotive and/or opinionated, perhaps by underlining these words.

Some examples of subjective vocabulary, phrases, clauses and statements are:

- emotive language (e.g. shaven-headed thug, work-shy, troublemaker);

- stereotypes and generalisations (e.g. tea-drinking English, famine-ravaged Africa, youth, the elderly, the disabled);

- persuading words and phrases (e.g. surely, obviously, as everyone knows).

b)

- Now read an article from the same journal or newspaper.

- Compose your own list of the differences in the language and presentation.

Critical analysis

Critical analysis is the key feature tutors/lecturers are looking for in your assignments. It involves thinking about issues and evaluating them. It is sometimes interpreted by students as the opposite of just describing something, but it is much more than that. Instead of describing, offer objective explanations, evidence and evaluation for why certain things are said or done. It is also important that you relate theory to practice both as a trainee teacher and as a student of education.

Critical analysis is derived from two words. 'Critical' comes from the Greek *'kriticos'*, meaning to discern and separate [the issues]. 'Analysis' comes from the French *'analyser'*, meaning to undo.

Objectivity means standing back and weighing the evidence even if you disagree with something. You can remain objective by examining the positive and negative aspects of all issues, evaluating a selection of different theories on issues and using the third person instead of first person. However, as a great deal of your writing (particularly as a trainee teacher or educational practitioner) will involve reflecting upon and analysing your own practice, you will write predominantly in the first person.

Examples written in the first person: *I think this happens because. . .*; *In my opinion. . .*

Example written in the third person: *The evidence suggests this happens because. . .*

Good critical analysis is not simply about writing. It is also about thinking critically. Before you start any assignment, you need to be clear about your focus. At university this usually means thinking critically about the requirements of the assignment.

Writing academic discourses involves using critical thinking skills to analyse a problem or issue. Imagine that you have to write an essay in which you are to analyse an issue and explain your view. This requires critical thinking skills.

Critical thinking and analysis in assignment writing

How do you know what is expected of you when you start to write an assignment?

The following suggestions are essential if you are to understand any assignment brief:

- Read your programme/course handbook.

- Read your unit/module handbooks. (They are your starting point for thinking about what is expected of you in assignments.)

- Look at the key skills you are required to develop.

- Find the page that tells you how to set out your assignments.

- Read the learning objectives for your weekly sessions at university.

- Define the performance level descriptors.

- Answer the following questions: 'What am I learning on this module/programme?' and 'How can I show this in my assignments?'

- Do not wait until your first assignment deadline is near. Start thinking ahead!

In order to answer your assignment question fully, you need to analyse the demands of the question. Assignment questions contain direction words. Verbs are crucial in telling you how you should answer the question. It is vital that you understand these as they help you to formulate analysis and discussion in your assignments. Below are some definitions, but there are many more of these in study guides.

Some definitions of examples of vocabulary used in assignment titles and examination questions

Vocabulary	Explanations
Account for	Give reasons for
Analyse	Break an issue or problem into parts and discuss each part objectively, giving a variety of arguments and evidence.
Argue	Support or reject a position by presenting reasons and evidence for and against each position.
Comment on	Use evidence to explain why something is or is not important.
Compare	Show the way things are alike and explain why.
Contrast	Show the way things are not alike and explain why.
Critically evaluate	Objectively give your judgement about whether something is important or not important, relevant or irrelevant or effective or ineffective. Give examples and evidence for your reasons.

Define	Give the precise meaning or offer different meanings for the same thing.
Discuss	Investigate by looking at all sides of the issue(s).
Evaluate/ assess	Decide how valuable, important or effective something is or is not. Address any weaknesses.
Explain	Give reasons for why something does or does not happen.
Illustrate	Use clear examples and/or case studies to explain something.
Outline	Give the main features, principles, events, etc.

Adapted from Assignment Guidance, Edgehill University Faculty of Education

You will often be given a list of factors to consider in your assignment guidelines. Do not assume this is a ready-made plan. Sometimes the list is not in any particular order and is only there to guide you. Try cutting the list up and moving the points around to help you make a structured plan. If in doubt, check with your tutor.

An assignment brief

Critically examine the key values underpinning a multi-professional approach to the Every Child Matters agenda in educational establishments. Illustrate your discussion with reference to specific aspects of practice.

Tips

- Highlight the direction words (e.g. 'critically examine' and 'illustrate') in one colour.

- Highlight other key words (e.g. 'values', 'multi-professional' and 'practice') in different colours.

- Brainstorm on paper or use a software package such as *Inspiration* to help you map your ideas (e.g. list all the agencies who might impact on a child's life and the values which you consider are important such as confidentiality).

- Rewrite the question in your own words (e.g. 'Examine in a critical manner the central issues which I understand make multi-professional working important in providing for and protecting children, making reference to any practice I might have observed.') to help you understand it.

- Try to break the question down (e.g. 'What is a multi-professional approach?', 'What is the Every Child Matters agenda?', 'What are educational establishments?' and 'What are the key values?').

Planning your assignments

- Break down the question.

- Brainstorm.

- Read your course notes.

- Do your extra research.

- Allocate words to each section.

- Do an outline plan.

- Draft, re-draft, and edit.

- Proofread!

Worked example

Below is a worked example which demonstrates the stages a student undertook when answering the following assignment.

Critically examine the education professional's role in promoting language diversity in the classroom. In particular, consider the issues related to the immersion/bilingualism debate. Provide a detailed analysis of how children who have English as an additional language can be supported in their learning, making reference to a child or group of children you have worked with in school or nursery.

Here are four steps that helped the student in thinking through their answer:

(These do not make a definitive model but are one way of approaching the task.)

1. Identify your initial view and why you hold it. Writing out your initial ideas will help clarify your thoughts. To do this you must read critically in order to identify and explore the evidence within the literature.

    For example:

    a) You would start from your own experiences and knowledge base such as any classroom experiences you may have had. Below are the student's initial thoughts as they started this assignment:

Last year I worked in a nursery which had a large proportion of children who had been in the country for less than a year. Because their English was so limited and they struggled with what they were asked to do, I thought it would have been a good idea to withdraw these children from working and playing with their peers and be given small group tuition in English.

    b) Below is a selection of resources which the student read and accessed to increase knowledge and understanding of the central issue:

    Crosse, K. (2007) *Introducing English as an additional language to young children: a practical handbook*. London: Heinemann.

    Scott, C. (2008) *Teaching children English as an additional language*. London: Taylor & Francis Ltd.

    Editorial Team Teachernet, last updated May 2007, available at www.teachernet.gov.uk/teachingandlearninglibrary/EALteaching, accessed January 2009.

2. Seek other views and more evidence. Make sure you examine all sides, especially those that are contrary to your ideas or what you have observed in, for example, your practice. Consult people who have expertise in the topic.

    For example:

After reading Gregory (1997), I realised the disadvantages in withdrawing children from their English-speaking peers. Instead I now believe that it would be much better to focus on speaking and listening learning experiences which included all the children to enable the non-English speakers to learn from their peers as well as adults.

3. Evaluate the evidence using valid criteria, which will be determined by your framework of evaluation. Construct a chart with points that are in agreement and disagreement. Then compare these with your initial view. Present evidence to support your discussion/argument.

    For example:

    You will now need to read some specific texts to help you reflect on the appropriateness of your initial views of:

    'speaking and listening experiences which would enable the non-English speakers to learn from their peers as well as their teachers'

    Editorial Team Teachernet, last updated May 2007, available at www.teachernet.gov.uk/teachingandlearning/library/EALteaching, accessed January 2009.

    Gregory, E. (1997) *One child, many worlds: early learning in multicultural communities.* London: David Fulton.

    Hall, D. (1995) *Assessing the needs of bilingual pupils: living in two languages.* London: David Fulton.

    Judge, B.C. (2003) Chapter 9 in Crawford, K, (ed) *Contemporary Issues in education: an introduction.* Dereham: Peter Francis.

    Porter, B. (2004) *Understanding each other: supporting children with English as an additional language (EAL) in early years settings.* Chester: Cheshire County Council.

4. Construct a balanced argument. Your challenge is to develop a response you consider the most logical in the light of the evidence available to you. This will be a synthesis of the information you have researched from multiple perspectives and your initial ideas on the issue.

An example of how to record a balanced argument to inform your discourse

Withdrawal from English-speaking peers		Working alongside English-speaking peers	
Resource	Argument	Resource	Argument
		Judge B	Inclusion means that all pupils should be offered the same opportunities and that true integration enables children to learn from one another.

Summary of key points

Define the problem carefully and completely.

Listen to and investigate all sides of an issue.

Be willing to change a position when shown reasons and evidence.

Seek alternative solutions in an attempt to choose the best solution.

Realise that the best is not the same for everyone.

Remain open to others' values and opinions.

Question and compare conflicting interpretations of data.

Evaluate conclusions.

References and further reading

Browne, M.N. and Keeley, S.M. (2009) *Asking the right questions: a guide to critical thinking*. Harlow: Pearson Education.

Cottrell, S. (2005) *Critical thinking skills*. Basingstoke: Palgrave Macmillan.

Crosse, K. (2007) *Introducing English as an additional language to young children: a practical handbook*. Oxford: Heinemann.

Donaldson, M. (1984) *Children's Minds*. London: Fontana

Douglas, J.W.B. (1964) *The home and school*. London: MacGibbon and Kee.

Gregory, E. (1997) *One child, many worlds: early learning in multicultural communities*. London: David Fulton.

Hall, D. (1995) *Assessing the needs of bilingual pupils: living in two languages*. London: David Fulton.

Judge, B.C. (2003) Chapter 9 in Crawford, K. (ed) *Contemporary issues in education: an introduction*. Dereham: Peter Francis.

Piaget, J. (1972) *The child's conception of the world*. Towota, NJ: Littlefield Adams.

Porter, B. (2004) *Understanding each other: supporting children with English as an additional language (EAL) in early years settings*. Chester: Cheshire County Council.

Scott, C. (2008) *Teaching children English as an additional language*. London: Taylor & Francis Ltd.

Teacher Net Editorial Team (2007) www.teachernet.gov.uk/teachingand learninglibrary/EALteaching, accessed January 2009.

2. A critical thinking community

Introduction

In this chapter you will explore the ways in which you can develop your critical thinking skills in collaboration with others. A range of particular skills is required in order to work effectively in a collaborative way. Some of these skills you will need to bring to the experience, while others you will develop as you become more experienced in the approach.

Learning outcomes

Having worked through this chapter you should be better able to:

- recognise the value of working with others to develop your thinking;

- make use of a range of skills for working collaboratively;

- contribute to the learning of others.

Working collaboratively

Many programmes of study will include opportunities for learning in collaboration with others, rather than in isolation. Students may be set investigative tasks which need to be done as a group, or they will be asked to present their work in a group presentation. For many students this may be a new experience. It takes time to move from studying by oneself to working with others. Clearly there will be tensions as well as opportunities, and it is worth considering how you will handle these tensions in order to establish the best atmosphere for everyone's learning.

Reflective task

Reflect back on your educational journey thus far.

- How many opportunities have you had to work collaboratively?

- Do you feel you work well within a group?

- Have you found collaborative working to be effective?

- What reservations might you have about working collaboratively?

Value of learning communities

Learning collaboratively makes use of an embedded human trait which recognises that we are dependent on one another and need to work as a team to be effective. None of us can expect to know everything there is to know about one subject or possess all the skills required to fulfil a task. Each of us brings our own life experiences, values and perspectives to each endeavour.

Within an educational context, working collaboratively recognises that we are all working within a similar framework. It is likely that we will all be tackling similar tasks. Therefore, it makes sense for us to consider challenges together. The group members we are working with will bring to the discussion their individual experiences of education, children, educational institutions, families and the work place. Some group members may have specialised in particular subjects such as child development, Special Educational Needs (SEN), specific school curriculum subjects, etc. Working collaboratively offers the opportunity for each of us to share these experiences and expertise, and learn from those of others in the group.

Reflective task

Think about your work in education thus far. Make a list of experiences, knowledge, skills, values and attitudes that you are able to bring to a collaborative study group. Identify when and where you developed these attributes.

The challenges of working collaboratively

Sometimes you will hear people referred to as 'good team workers'. This usually indicates that they are comfortable working collaboratively in a particular environment. However, working in this way is not without its challenges. Some of us are indeed comfortable with collaboration, but some of us are less confident with it. Some of us are used to relying on ourselves to address tasks and prefer to work independently. This can make us resistant to collaboration as we are unsure that we can trust other members of the group in the way that we trust ourselves.

Some of the advantages of working collaboratively can also be seen as disadvantages. For example, each of us seeing things from a different perspective also means that we may not agree on certain matters. It is important to be aware of these challenges as you embark on collaborative work so that potential difficulties can be anticipated and, hopefully, minimised.

Practical task

Divide a page in half and consider the advantages and disadvantages of working collaboratively. Discuss with a colleague how you might overcome the challenges.

The Action Learning Set process

The concept of Action Learning Sets is attributed to Reg Revans (1998) who developed it as a way of improving shared learning within organisations. It is considered to be a valuable way of developing a collaborative approach in which peers can share their own learning and contribute to the learning of others.

There are several ways of operating Action Learning Sets, depending on the aims of the Sets and what they are trying to achieve. For the purposes of this chapter, Action Learning Sets will offer a way for students working in a similar field (e.g. education) to develop their critical thinking skills in collaboration with others who are working on similar projects.

The aim of the Set is to forward each individual's thinking in order that they can put something into practice more effectively. Thinking and action are thus equal partners. The group meets on a regular basis throughout an identified period, perhaps three months, to share their work, thoughts and problems.

Action Learning Sets involve participants in 're-imaging' their experiences through the process of sharing them with others. Each member of the group offers their experiences and perspectives to the rest of the group in order to gain new insight into them. The group is invited to respond to each member's experiences in order to help them better understand those experiences and identify possible strategies for future action.

Action Learning Sets encourage us to be open to new ways of seeing and interpreting our experiences, welcome the perspective of others and value the challenges to our own assumptions. They can help us to clarify our thinking and narrow down the real concerns that underpin our interest in an area.

Establishing the Set

Action Learning Sets are usually made up of between four and seven people. These numbers are considered to be small enough to ensure contributions from a variety of perspectives but are not so large as to inhibit people or prevent people from having the opportunity to contribute.

The Sets are usually composed of people who have a common interest; group members are familiar with the world in which each other is operating. Sets could contain people who know each other well or who are complete strangers. You may wish to consider the advantages and disadvantages of both ways of working. Practical considerations may also come into play. For example, are all participants able to meet at a particular time and place?

Identifying goals

Early in the formation of the Set, the group members need to identify what they hope to achieve by working together. This will depend on whether the group has a shared concern or whether they have formed their Set using other criteria, such as friendship groups. A shared concern can be more valuable as the Set members are likely to be pondering the same issues, reading similar material and trying out similar strategies in the practice context.

Establishing rules of operation

It is important that the Set is clear about the expectations of all participants. The group needs to agree on how they plan to operate, when and where they will meet and what rules they need to follow in order to work effectively. Early in the process the group might wish to develop their own guidelines for working together. They might also consider what they will do if a member of the group does not follow the guidelines. For example, will someone else in the group take them to task over it?

Roles of participants

The group may decide to allocate certain roles to each participant. Some Action Learning Sets have a facilitator who is external to the group (e.g. a university tutor) and some are self-facilitating. Some groups may nominate a scribe or a discussion leader. Such roles also need to be clarified, and could be rotated around the group over the weeks.

A typical Action Learning Set meeting

Once the aims and rules of the Action Learning Set have been established, the next meeting will need to encourage participants to share their initial areas of interest or concern. Prior to this meeting, participants might be asked to bring their concern or issue, perhaps as a piece of writing, to the meeting. During the meeting, all members of the Action Learning Set might be given the opportunity to share their issue or concern to establish the range of issues brought to the group. The meeting might include:

*   reviewing notes taken at the last meeting;

*   sharing written work generated by the group;

*   focusing on one or more members' work;

*   discussing one point of concern to all the group;

*   questioning of some/all members' work;

*   giving verbal/written feedback to members;

*   documenting the meeting;

*   generating action points to bring to the next meeting;

*   agreeing on the focus of the next meeting.

At the end of the meeting, all members should be given a task to do in preparation for the next meeting

Working effectively

Developing the skills to work in this way takes time and commitment. Many of us – especially in education – are prone to talking rather than listening. The development of effective listening skills is crucial to this process. This means resisting the temptation to interrupt, trying to anticipate what a group member will say next or jumping in with your own anecdote. It means using active listening skills which attempt to hear not only what the person is saying, but what lies behind their words. It also means allowing silent spaces to enable the speaker to think and giving them enough uninterrupted time to finish what they want to say.

Reflective task

What might you learn about someone from listening to them speak about their work?

Questioning skills are also central to the process. Such questioning might involve asking for clarification, unpacking assumptions and challenging contradictions or faulty reasoning. Open questions, which allow the respondent to elaborate on points and share their perspective, are preferable to closed questions, which shut down speculation.

Having listened to a member of the Set, you may wish to ask questions which:

* clarify what they have said – *Are you saying that. . .?*;

* challenge what they have said – *What do you mean by. . .?*, *Why is that important?* or *How is that significant?*;

* unpack terms and concepts – *What do you understand by the term. . .?*;

* ask for evidence from experiences – *Can you give me an example of when. . .?*;

- suggest a different interpretation of events – *Is it possible that. . .?*, *Could it be that..?* or *What if. . .?*;

- seek justifications for their views – *How do you know that. . .?* or *What evidence is there for. . .?*;

- link their thoughts to future practice – *If this is the case, what might you need to do?*.

We need to avoid putting our own views and interpretations onto the speaker. We would *not* want to:

- shift the focus to our own areas of interest;

- say what we would have done in a similar situation;

- attempt to give answers to the questions;

- offer suggestions of how they may operate in future;

- enter into an argument in order to exert power.

However, we also have responsibilities as the speaker. Speakers also have skills to learn. We should ensure that we:

- speak as clearly and concisely as possible;

- avoid too much anecdotal evidence;

- be prepared to substantiate claims;

- do not assume a shared understanding of terms and concepts;

- avoid giving simple explanations of events;

- dwell on past experiences which can no longer be changed;

- anticipate future practice.

Each member of the Action Learning Set should leave a meeting feeling that they have been able to contribute to others' learning and have taken away something for their own learning. The meeting should leave each member feeling confident in their own expertise and curious about the next stage of their investigation. They should be clear about the expectations of the next meeting and what they need to do to prepare for it.

Worked example

Action Learning Set members had each brought a piece of writing to their meeting. They had agreed that they would read each others' work with a view to identifying questions which might help move their thinking on. All the pieces of writing were circulated around the five members of the group. Each person added to the questions raised by the previous readers. Eventually, each member received their own piece of writing back. One particular group member was interested to note that one section of their work had generated a lot of questions from his colleagues. The section read:

The children appear to have no interest in school. I guess that's not surprising, because their parents don't seem to be interested either.

Among the questions this small comment had generated were the following:

- How do you know that the parents aren't interested?

- How do children show their lack of interest?

- What other reasons could there be for children's lack of interest?

- What makes you think it is the parents' attitudes that is influencing them?

- What influence do parents' attitudes have over their children's?

- Are you saying that nothing can be done to get children interested in school?

- Even if the parents lack interest, what are you going to do to educate these children?

- Why would parents not be interested in what their children do in school?

Looking at the questions, the group member realised that they had made a lot of assumptions about the children they had met and their parents, whom they had not met. The group member took each of the questions offered by their group and began to try to answer them, reflecting on their own experiences, values and attitude and reading about the role of parents in children's education.

Summary of key points

Working collaboratively makes demands of and furthers your critical thinking skills.

Working in this way has its advantages and challenges.

A clear structure is needed for collaborative working.

Collaborative working can give us the confidence to explore our own critical skills through encountering those of others.

The process gives us the opportunity to contribute to the learning of others.

References and further reading

Etherington, K. (2004) *Becoming a reflexive researcher: using our selves in research*. London: Jessica Kingsley.

Fry, H., Ketteridge, S. and Marshall, S. (2000) *A Handbook for teaching and learning in higher education*. London: Kogan Page.

McGill, I. and Beaty A. (2000) *Action learning: a guide for professional management and educational development* (2nd edition). London: Kogan Page.

McGill, I. and Brockbank, A. (2004) *The action learning handbook*. London: Routledge Falmer.

O'Neil, V.J.,and Marsick, J. (2007) *Understanding action learning*. New York: AMACOM.

Revans, R. (1998) *ABC of action learning* (3rd Edition). London: Lemos and Crane.

3. Analysing a placement context

Introduction

A significant part of any course of study which is designed to prepare students for a specific profession will usually involve periods of study in a work context. Such placements are designed to give you experience of what being a member of the profession will be like and enable you to put into practice some of the work you have been doing in college or university.

Even though such places serve similar purposes and work towards similar goals, it becomes very apparent that they are all different and have their own distinctive features. The reasons for these differences are many and varied, and it is important that you recognise the implications of these differences for your work in each context. You need to be able to critically evaluate your own responses to each context and decide how you will need to work within each context.

Learning outcomes

Having worked through this chapter you should be better able to:

- critically analyse the features of a placement context;

- develop your critical thinking skills in relation to placement contexts;

- use your critical thinking skills to modify your practice.

The significance of context for professional development

Any professional programme of study must recognise that an individual's performance is substantially affected by the context in which they operate. No amount of classroom study can ever prepare a student for the infinite variety of what they may come across in the work context. Sometimes, there may be the temptation for students on professional programmes to ask their tutors to tell them the right way to do something. The truth is that there is no 'right' way to do it, because anything that we choose to do in a work context must take into account the particular demands, priorities, opportunities and limitations offered by a particular place.

The significance of context is related to the opportunities you will have to develop certain aspects of your professional development. You therefore need to analyse each new context in order to identify which aspects you will have the opportunity to focus on.

Not only does a consideration of context reveal opportunities to develop aspects of your professional development, it also offers a significant strategy for learning. This is because you can consider your work in the context as data, which you can legitimately use to contribute to your understanding of aspects of your professional expertise. As you gather information about the context, you build a bank of data that you can analyse at a later time to track how you are relating and responding to that context.

This rich ongoing data can then be scrutinised in the light of your other studies (e.g. reading, university lectures and seminars and conversations with colleagues). Your analysis can help you to synthesise the different data sources to build a more useful picture of your professional work.

Reflective task

Review your own professional development thus far. Which areas do you feel you have made progress in? Which areas do you feel you still need to work on or have experience of? Make a list of your next five priorities for development. Consider how context might affect your ability to address these areas. For example:

Priority 1: I would like to have more experience of working with children who are learning English as an additional language (EAL).

Importance of context: The context would need to have children who are learning EAL.

The process of contextual analysis

In order to make the best use of contextual analysis, it is important to plan for it as carefully as you might plan for any other aspect of your work. This means being alert to information from the beginning of your time in the particular context and having a strategy to process this information.

Initial analysis

Before you even arrive at your new placement setting, you will begin to build a picture of what it will be like. The very name of the institution will provide indicators of the setting. For example, you might safely assume that a school called 'St Matthews C of E' has a Church of England foundation and is likely to have Christianity as a reference point. You may also begin to formulate some view of the place because of its location (e.g. inner city or rural).

Information about the context may also be available from external sources, such as the local authority (LA), OFSTED, or family and friends who know the place. It is useful to gather this data as a starting point for getting to know the context. However, we must exercise caution here. It is very easy to jump to conclusions based on very little information or indeed information that is influenced by someone else's view. We need to examine this initial data to begin to understand our own perspectives. Our interpretation of this data may tell us far more about ourselves than the place we seek to understand.

You will continue this process of initial analysis from the moment you arrive at the premises. From the outside you will absorb features of the location, of the school, building and grounds. As you enter the building you will notice the layout, decor, displays and signs.

Each of these will begin to give you an idea of the philosophy, values and priorities of the place. How that institution chooses to use its buildings, furniture and resources will give you insight into what it considers important. Alongside this process you will also need to analyse why you have interpreted certain features in a particular way. This will again give you an insight into your own philosophy, values and priorities.

Reflective task

What might the following features tell you about a school?

What might your answers tell you about yourself?

- All doors are locked, there are bars on the windows and the main entrance is controlled by an intercom system.

- On the outside of the building there are no signs indicating where the entrance is.

- In the school grounds there is what looks like an allotment and a pond.

- In the playground there is an area with seating, potted plants and a sign which says 'Friendship station'.

- In the playground outside each classroom there is a covered area with benches, tables and a chalk board.

- In the main entrance of the school, the reception desk is an open area with soft chairs and children's work and information about the staff on display.

- Along the corridor one door is labelled 'Family room'. It contains soft chairs and facilities for making tea and coffee.

- All displays along the corridor have text written in English and at least two other languages.

Some features of a particular context will have a direct impact on how you will operate; some features may be more important to you than others. It may be unrealistic to try to respond to every distinctive feature, and so your next task is to prioritise. You need to ask yourself which features will offer you the best opportunity for professional development.

The number of choices you make will depend on the amount of time you have on placement, and you should be realistic in what you wish to achieve. You might wish to discuss your ambitions with an experienced colleague. Once you have identified your key issues, you need to unpack each issue in detail. You can do this by asking yourself a series of questions:

- Why have I chosen this area as a key issue?

- What have I noticed about this issue in this context?

- Why is it important for my professional development?

- What concerns do I have about my own expertise in this area?

- What would I like to achieve by the end of the placement?

- How will I know whether I have been successful?

Your answers to these questions should form a descriptive narrative which will help you to articulate your thoughts, feelings and intentions. Doing this should give you a sense of where you would like to get to during the time of the placement.

Practical task

Make a list of all the different types of play that children in a nursery setting might engage in. Select a number of these which you might target over a four-week placement. For each one, give reasons why that type of play might be a focus. What questions might you ask about each one?

Continuing analysis

Once targets have been established, the process of analysis continues on a regular basis throughout your time in the context. Some people find it useful to analyse developments on a daily basis, while others prefer a weekly basis. You might wish to consider the benefits of each approach.

For any focus, you must first decide what kind of data you need to collect. For example, you may have decided to observe children in a particular environment, without you becoming involved. The information or data that you collect could be in the form of one or several of the following:

- written notes which you jot down as you observe;

- completed structured observation schedules;

- photographs;

- recordings.

It is important to ensure that written notes are purely descriptive, without any attempt to interpret what you see. In the practical task below, your attention is drawn to the first stage of the process and the need for neutral description.

Practical task

a) Compare the two sets of observation notes below:

Account 1:

> *Thomas and Christie were messing about in the home area. They showed little interest in the resources and preferred to throw them around rather than play with them.*

Account 2:

> *Thomas picked up a doll and threw it on the floor. Christie said 'Don't do that' and put it in the cot. She then picked up a cup and threw it at Thomas, saying 'You don't throw babies'. Thomas said, 'I don't want to play with dolls anyway'.*

Consider the following:

- What features are similar in both accounts?

- What features are different?

- In what ways is Account 1 more of an interpretation of events than Account 2?

- What do we learn about the children in each account?

- Which account is most useful to the practitioner? Why?

b) Immediately following the observation notes, we need to consider the questions it raises for us. For example, why did Thomas throw the doll?

Practical task continued

Does he not like playing in the home area? Does he dislike dolls? Does he not want to play with Christie? Make a list of other questions this event might raise.

c) Identify possible areas of study from this exchange. For example, why do boys and girls play with different toys in this nursery?

A note on ethical issues

Any work that involves collecting information about others, whether from adults or children, needs to be in line with the ethical procedures set out by the programmes which you are studying. You must ensure that the work you do meets the requirements which are designed to protect not only anonymity, but individuals from exploitation.

Worked example

A student was on her second main placement as part of her study to become a primary teacher. A key feature of the school where she worked was that many of the children were learning EAL (English as an Additional Language). In her initial analysis she had identified three things that she planned to do to develop her skills in this area. These were to:

1 Observe a class teacher working with individual learners of EAL.

2 Read about EAL.

3 Consider the needs of the children who are learning EAL in all my lesson plans.

Using these strategies, she hoped that by the end of her placement she would achieve her target of 'developing confidence in working with children who are learning EAL'.

The student devised an observation schedule that she could use when the teacher was working with the class. The schedule divided the teacher's interaction with the children into sections:

- time of observation;

- activity;

- teacher's introduction;

- group work;

- individual work;

- end of lesson.

At each stage of the lesson the student looked at how the teacher adapted her language for learners, what resources she used, how she dealt with misunderstandings, how she used other children as support, how the lesson had been modified to suit particular learners, etc.

The student was able to take her observations and use them to draw up some principles for her own teaching and practical examples for her own lesson planning.

Reviewing professional development

Contextual analysis is cyclical in nature. That is, one set of questions will lead to investigation, which in turn may lead to further questions and investigation. During the course of any placement in a work-based context, several of these cycles may take place as you get to know the context better and discover more information. You may also find that issues that seemed important to you at the beginning of a placement become less important, and other features take on greater significance for your professional development. Do not be afraid to switch your focus in order to meet your own learning needs.

Towards the end of the placement you will want to review your progress in relation to your key issues. Of course, there will be a a great deal that you have learned about children and their development, the process of learning and yourself. However, it is important that you track what progress you have made in relation to those things which stood out as significant for you. You might wish to ask yourself the following series of questions:

- How has my thinking moved on in relation to my key issues?

- What do I know now that I did not before?

- How has this context developed my professional awareness and skills?

- How will it inform my future work with children?

- What issues will be among my next priorities?

Summary of key points

The critical thinking skills involved in learning from a specific context are ones which can easily be transferred to other areas of learning.

The skills involved in analysing a context are essential for any individual seeking to understand their role in the education and care of children.

Critical thinking skills involve careful observation and data gathering from the context, interpretation of complex environments and events and a level of self-analysis which reveals your own values and beliefs.

References and further reading

ABC of action learning (3rd edition) London: Lemos and Crane.

Anning, A. and Edwards, A. (2006) *Promoting children's learning from birth to five*. Buckinghamshire: Open University Press.

Arthur, J., Grainger, T., Wray, D. (2006) *Learning to teach in the primary school*. London: Routledge.

Edwards, A. and Talbot, R. (1999) *The hard-pressed researcher: a research handbook for the caring professions*. London: Longman.

Etherington, K. (2004) *Becoming a reflexive researcher: using our selves in research*. London: Jessica Kingsley.

Jacques, K. and Hyland, R. (eds) (2007) *Professional studies: primary and early years* (3rd edition). Exeter: Learning Matters.

4. Analysing data and interpreting findings

Introduction

In this chapter you will explore the collection of data, the subsequent analysis of that data, and how it informs your professional practice. You will begin to understand that when analysing any data you have collected and/or when considering data that others have collected, you will need to apply the critical thinking skills you have developed in the previous chapters.

Learning outcomes

Having worked through this chapter you should be better able to understand:

- **the different types of data available to you;**

- **how to interpret that data and use it in your writing.**

Different types of data and its analysis

There are fundamentally two distinctive types of data which can be collected, collated and analysed. These are quantitative data and qualitative data.

Quantitative data

- Quantitative data is the collation of facts which provide data that is measured or identified on a numerical scale.

- Quantitative research techniques generate a mass of numbers that need to be summarised, described and analysed.

- Characteristics of quantitative data may be described and explored by drawing graphs and charts, doing cross tabulations and calculating mean and standard deviations.

- Further analysis will build on these initial findings, seeking patterns and relationships in the data by comparing means, exploring correlations and performing multiple regressions or analyses of variance.

- Advanced modelling techniques may eventually be used to build sophisticated explanations of how the data addresses the original question.

- Although methods used can vary greatly, the following steps are common in quantitative data analysis:

  1   identify a data entry and analysis manager (e.g. SPSS, a predictive analysis company);

  2   review data (e.g. surveys, questionnaires, etc.) for completeness;

  3   code data;

  4   enter data;

  5   analyse data using other statistical tests.

The collection of quantitative data is a long process which, at this stage of your development, can deflect from your long-term goal of developing the skills of critical analysis. Quantitative data is best reserved for longitudinal research programmes. Because of the size of the samples in the types of small-scale research you are likely to be involved in, it would be difficult to justify considered conclusions which could be applied to the field.

Qualitative data

- Qualitative data analysis describes and summarises the mass of words generated by interviews or observational data.

- Qualitative data allows researchers to seek relationships between various themes that have been identified or relate behaviour or ideas to biographical characteristics of respondents.

- Implications for policy or practice may be derived from qualitative data or interpretation may be sought of puzzling findings from previous studies.

- Ultimately, theory could be developed and tested using advanced analytical techniques.

- Although methods of analysis can vary greatly, the following 11 steps are typical for qualitative data analysis:

  1 become familiar with the data through repeated reading, listening, etc;

  2 transcribe interviews, etc;

  3 record observations within a contex;

  4 organise and index data for easy retrieval and identification;

  5 anonymise sensitive data;

  6 code (or index) data;

  7 identify themes;

  8 develop provisional categories;

  9 explore relationships between categories;

  10 refine themes and categories;

  11 develop theory and incorporate pre-existing knowledge.

The collection of qualitative data is probably the type of data gathering which you are more likely to be engaged in while on a degree course which is concerned with educational issues. This type of data is often collected while undertaking some form of ethnographic research. So what is ethnographic research and why is it important in the disciplines you are studying?

Ethnography is defined as the descriptive study of a particular human society or group. Contemporary ethnography is based almost entirely on fieldwork. An ethnographer works among the people who are the subject of study for a period of time, striving to maintain a degree of objective detachment. An ethnographer usually cultivates close relationships with informants who can provide specific information on aspects of the way of life and behaviour in certain contexts. While detailed written notes are the mainstay of fieldwork, ethnographers may also use tape recorders, cameras or video recorders. Figure 4.1 describes a cycle which represents the process undertaken in ethnographic research.

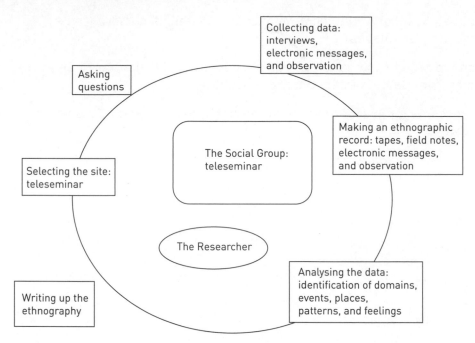

Figure 4.1 **The ethnographic research cycle**

Ethnographic research has broad implications for many fields, including education. Professional development evaluators and staff developers can use this approach to understand teachers' needs, experiences, viewpoints and goals. Such information can enable them to design useful and worthwhile programmes for teachers and ultimately improve student learning.

According to Spradley (1979), ethnography is 'the work of describing a culture' (p. 3). The goal of ethnographic research is 'to understand another way of life from the native point of view' (p. 3). Although this approach is commonly used by anthropologists to study exotic cultures and primitive societies, Spradley suggests that it is a useful tool for 'understanding how other people see their experience' (p. iv). He emphasises, however, that 'rather than studying people, ethnography means learning from people' (p. 3).

So, as discussed in Chapter 3, you can see that the observations and data you collect during any worked-based placement you may undertake will probably fall under the umbrella of ethnographic research.

Interpreting data

The interpretation of any data which you collect should be grounded in your initial study hypotheses, theory or research questions. Therefore, when you examine the data you must recognise the following issues:

- Data interpretation methods vary greatly depending on the theoretical focus (i.e. qualitative or quantitative research and the research methodology which you have followed).

- Ensure you understand relevant information on statistics. You should seek further advice for this step from computer package manuals (e.g. SPSS and Nvivo) and methodology books.

- The last step of data analysis consists of interpreting the findings to see whether they support your initial study hypotheses, theory or research questions.

Practical task

SAT results

Percentage of pupils achieving level 4 or above in SAT tests for English, Mathematics and Science

Local authority	English	Mathematics	Science
North West	82	80	89
Blackburn with Darwen	81	79	88
Blackpool	78	79	87
Bolton	79	78	86
Bury	84	81	89
Cheshire	84	81	90
Cumbria	84	82	90
Halton	84	81	92
Knowsley	79	76	89
Lancashire	81	80	88
Liverpool	79	76	86
Manchester	74	74	84
Oldham	80	79	87

Practical task continued

Rochdale	78	78	88
Salford	80	78	87
Sefton	86	83	93
St. Helens	83	80	91
Stockport	87	84	92
Tameside	82	79	90
Trafford	86	85	92
Warrington	85	84	91
Wigan	83	81	90
Wirral	85	79	91

What conclusion can you draw from the above statistics?

Which LA has the overall best performance?

Table 4.1 **Table of SATs results by regions**

Reflective task

Below is an account of an incident which occurred during a student teacher's school-based training. This record is a piece of evidence and as such can be treated as part of the student's research data about the context of their placement.

Entering the room with a great deal of noise, the child throws himself into his chair and folds his arms.

Teacher: Why have you been sent back?

Child: For nuffin'. I din't do nuffin'.

Teacher: You must have done something. Everyone says they didn't do anything.

Child: What's the poin' anyway? I 'ate school, you only ever get told off. I wish there weren't any school.

Teacher: But what would you do instead?

Child: Dunno.

Teacher: How would you earn a living? What would you do all day?

Child: I'd jus' play on me PlayStation and stuff.

Teacher: But if there wasn't school, how would a PlayStation have been invented? Where would you get a job to get the money to buy the games and the console?

Child begins to fidget and smile.

Child: I dunno. They jus' would be there.

Consider the following:

- What information can you elicit from this piece of data?

- Is this a specific type of research data? What makes you think this?

- How would the data assist you to make judgements about the context of this placement and the child in particular?

Summary of key points

Decide which type of data you are going to use. (Remember that different types of data provide different types of evidence.)

Use the data to either substantiate your theory or be willing to change a position when shown reasons and evidence.

Question and compare conflicting interpretations of data.

Evaluate conclusions.

References and further reading

Langdridge, D. and Hagger-Johnson, G. (2009) *Introduction to research methods and data analysis* (2nd edition). Harlow: Prentice Hall.

Rice-Lively, M.L. http://fiat.gslis.utexas.edu/~marylynn/index.html, accessed December 2008.

Smith, K., Todd, M. and Waldman, J. (2009) *Doing your undergraduate social science dissertation.* New York: Routledge.

Spradley, J.P. (1979) *The ethnographic interview.* New York: Holt, Rinehart, and Winston.

Viadero, D. (1996, June 12) Researchers seek new road map for teaching. *Education Week*, XV(38): 9.

5. Analysing your own writing

Introduction

In previous chapters you will have thought about how your critical thinking can be reflected in your writing. This chapter looks at the process of reviewing the writing itself and using analysis of your writing as a learning tool. This chapter guides you through checking the level of your criticality. It shows you how this criticality may be built into your writing. You will also analyse your own basic writing techniques.

Learning outcomes

Having worked through this chapter you should be better able to:

- reflect through writing (i.e. learn through writing and write reflectively);

- review the style and writing structure of your writing;

- consider the importance of the clerical tasks of editing and checking.

Thinking about your thinking . . . reflecting on your reflections . . . analysing your analysis

Reviewing your own writing is something that will be natural at a simple level. When writing an essay you will have reread sentences to check that they make sense. You will read whole paragraphs before moving on to the next section to ensure continuity. After a break you may read from the beginning to get yourself back into the flow of the writing. What you are less likely to do is analyse your own writing in order to reveal something about yourself professionally. This may require, as discussed in Chapter 1, that you are:

- willing to question your views;

- open to the ideas and views of others – just because something is in print does not mean it is true;

- able to give your (positive and negative) judgements;

- able to explore the implications of the evidence/literature;

- self-confident enough to explore the evidence presented;

- honest in facing your own biases/prejudices;

- flexible in considering alternatives and opinions;

- willing to reconsider and revise views where honest reflection suggests that change is warranted.

In Chapter 1 the words 'critical' and 'analysis' are defined. These definitions include aspects of separating out, revealing and clarifying. Sometimes there may be revelations not only of something that needs to change but also of something positive that strengthens your practice. This kind of criticality can happen in a different context. Earlier this text referred to reading your own writing critically as you were in the process of writing. Now it refers to writing critically about your own writing by self-referencing as a form of self-evaluation.

Worked example

The more familiar form of self-referencing is the straightforward use of quotations from a learning journal or a teaching file in a formal essay. In the following worked example a student teacher writes about their class teacher's use of one child with good EAL skills to support another child newly arrived in the class from Pakistan.

My teacher decided to seat Child A next to a bright child (Child B) who also originated from Pakistan and spoke both Urdu and English very well. It was explained to me that Child B could help with translating in the classroom as well as providing personal support to Child A throughout the school. As a new arrival, Child A needed to learn EAL as quickly as possible . . .

Following feedback from the assistant on Child A's English language development, my teacher started to give Child A the same set work as children in Wave 3 of the Primary National Strategy . . .

I, however, was concerned about . . . the onus on Child B to support Child A.

Looking back to notes in my journal (16/10/08) I noted:

> *'Child B speaks Urdu and has been helping Child A a lot but I sense that Child B is really getting fed up with it now as Child B has less time for their own work.'*

The impact of this extra responsibility was further evident when I came to mark Child B's report writing task for literacy. Child B is one of the top ability writers but this was not reflected in their work. I decided to speak to them . . . they then confided that they had not been able to concentrate as Child A was occupying a significant amount of their time asking questions. (Selina Webb, unpublished 2008)

The writer took a brief quote from their journal and then expanded on it in their essay, providing additional evidence to back up their view.

Suppose now that we consider how the student might take a more critical approach. They might have written that their 'sense' of something in the quotation '. . . but I sense that Child B is really getting fed up. . .' was initially left without the evidence that led to her supposition. The paragraph that follows does provide this evidence, but we do not know for certain what created the sense in the first place. To link the two would have provided a stronger logical flow to the writing. A critical style of writing might be as follows:

> *'Child B speaks Urdu and has been helping Child A a lot, but I sense that Child B is really getting fed up with it now as Child B has less time for their own work.'*

I believe the 'sense' that I had was not merely intuitive but was evidenced when I marked Child B's writing. Child B is one of the top ability writers but this was not reflected in her work.

This follow-up is critical in the sense of revealing more or making more evident (not in the sense of finding fault or shortcomings).

Reflective task

Find a self-quotation, perhaps from a journal or teaching file, in one of your essays.

Look critically at how it is used and decide if it has been reflected upon and considered critically or used as an illustration to support the point being made. Consider whether being more critical will add quality to your work or whether simply illustrating is exactly what the quotation needs to do.

Worked example

We will now look at an evaluation of an English lesson about the use of the prefixes 'un-' and 're-' which could be quoted in an essay about managing children's behaviour.

> *The children appeared more able to use the 'un-' prefix correctly than the 're-' prefix. I think that I pitched the level accurately but feel the children put less thought into their answers because of the presence of information and communication technology (ICT). As ICT facilitated the speed of task completion it appeared that the children were almost rushing to get through the activity. I believe that if this activity had been completed in written form then the children would have thought more thoroughly about the answers they were giving.*
>
> *As this was a small group session it was possible to provide one-to-one support, which enabled any technological difficulties about the activity to be overcome with ease.*
>
> ***The children appeared to enjoy the activity and behaved well.*** *They do need further support in recognising when to use the prefix 're-'. It will be necessary to repeat my lesson introduction next time to reinforce the meaning of 're-' as meaning 'again'. (Selina Webb, unpublished 2008)*

The bolded sentence is the one sentence that could be interesting to critically appraise. The student might quote the sentence and then challenge herself. She might write:

> *I have written about children enjoying themselves and behaving well in the same sentence. This implies that the latter is the consequence of the former, but the point is not fully clear. I think I meant that because the children were enjoying themselves, they behaved well. This would then support my belief that the general ethos of the classroom is the most significant factor in managing children's behaviour. . .*

Re-evaluation

The student went on to re-evaluate this experience and produced the following conclusion to her essay:

> *While at first I believed creating and maintaining a safe learning environment was about disciplining children to produce good behaviour, I now see there are many preventative steps that come prior to this that are concerned with the environment the children are in. Creating a positive working environment as described in this paper can reduce the likelihood of bad behaviour, and therefore reduce the need for discipline.*

The importance of writing in professional development is made most apparent when we realise that we can only reflect on or analyse our own thoughts if they have been recorded at one particular moment. Our thoughts are transient, developing all the time in response to experience, and they may be forgotten. To discover accurately how much we have moved on or to capture a bigger picture we need to record these frozen moments in our thinking history as best we can. Even the inaccuracies and the revealing of feelings that cloud the picture may be of interest if they tell us something about ourselves. Beveridge (1997, p. 33) notes that students need to 'reflect on (their) thoughts, check them against later experience, to refine them and improve them'.

Practical task

Think about how you evaluate your practice. Look at an example of how you have reflected on a session. Consider the following aspects:

- Were you able to describe a situation accurately with relevant detail that was problematic or could be improved even if the lesson worked well?

- Were you able to precisely identify any problems or strategies to improve in your practice?

- Did you discuss the problems with anyone? If so, consider what you learned from that discussion. Were you able to incorporate what others said into your writing?

- What form did your written evaluation take?

- What did you learn from that process of writing?

Now look in your later evaluations. Have you used that learning? Were you were able to further refine your understanding? If so, how?

Reflection

The term 'reflection' will be familiar to education students and student teachers. Frequently they will be required to reflect on their experiences as a means of learning. You will probably be familiar with the adage that a reflective practitioner learns from every experience, but the non-reflective practitioner will do the same things over and over again.

How does reflecting relate to analysis? Quite simply, analysis is part of the reflective process, but it is also a term that is applicable in other contexts. To start with, the word 'reflect' implies looking back. It will require thinking back to place yourself in the learning situation. It requires imagination to conjure up the detail. Considered in a reflective moment, the possible anxiety of the situation can be confronted and thought through. The term was first used in an educational context by the American academic Dewey (1933). The ideas were developed by Boud *et al.* (1985, pp. 26–31) in the form:

- 'returning to experience' – recalling or detailing important events;

- 'attending to feelings' – using helpful feelings and removing or managing obstructive ones;

- 'evaluating experience' – re-examining experience in the light of one's existing knowledge.

Practical task

Look at an essay or journal in which you have been required to reflect. Consider how you have addressed each of the three categories of reflection and whether there is a good balance in emphasis between them. Note that description is a necessary part of the process of revisiting the examined situation, but it needs to be selective and accurate. Good, relevant detail is valuable and feelings may offer important insights.

Levels of reflectiveness

A set of descriptions of levels of reflectiveness is useful when self-assessing written work that is reflective in character. Kember, McKay, Sinclair and Kam Yuet Wong (2008, pp. 369–79) propose four graded categories for assessing reflectiveness:

1. Habitual action

Expert practitioners do this in routine situations which they have met many times before. Students may follow rigidly a procedure that they have been taught (the student may then provide material in an essay without any sense of the meaning).

2. Understanding

In this case the student will demonstrate understanding of the technique or strategy but will have difficulty in applying it because it remains a theoretical concept. In writing, the explanation will show understanding but not how it might be used in practice. It has not become part of the student's working practice.

3. Reflection

Reflection requires that the student can relate concepts and ideas to their own experience. In written work, ideas will be illustrated appropriately with examples from the student's own practice.

4. Critical reflection

Critical reflection implies a change or transformation of perspective. When practice has become habitual this is more challenging. Students new to the practice will be more open to the possibility of change. This requires the student to recognise their own assumptions and to critically review them.

Practical task

Look at the same piece of reflective writing as in the last task and decide, as objectively as possible, which reflectiveness level it matches. Your judgement should be on a best-fit basis. You may find it helpful to isolate paragraphs and analyse them separately.

Reviewing style and writing structure

Some readers may have developed confidence in structuring their writing. However, this section addresses those who are uncertain and offers approaches to reviewing how writing may be put together.

In the field of education there are a number of approaches to writing that are commonly expected. You will be used to framing your writing with an introduction and a conclusion. The following section looks at the essential features of these structural elements.

The introduction

Generally, an introduction briefly sets out what you intend to cover in the essay. In essays that have a very non-specific brief that requires you to select an aspect of your own practice to explore, it becomes necessary to clarify your choice. The title 'A critical analysis of the potential for cross-curricular teaching and learning in foundation subjects' would be followed by an instruction to select one or a group of subjects as a focus for the discussion. The introduction would then outline why such subjects were chosen, which cross-curricular themes are to be included, and a reference to any general findings that might follow. There might well be an expectation that the student's own experience of teaching or observing the subjects being taught would be analysed and subjected to questioning. In response to the instruction 'Submit a piece of writing reflecting your personal response to the way an aspect of one of the tasks carried out in school has raised questions about your own practice', the following student clarifies not only the fact that their topic is cultural inclusion, but also from where they are drawing their examples and the fact that they are adopting a critical approach:

> *'Children from ethnic minority backgrounds now form a tenth of the pupil population' (Leung, 2001, p. 1). Given this fact, I realised the significance of inclusive practices and the embracing of all cultures during my first primary school placement. What I was not prepared for was the introduction of a seven-year-old boy into my Year 3 class who had just moved from Pakistan with no prior exposure to the English language.*

> *In this piece of writing I will analyse my class teacher's practice, both positive and less so, in handling this situation . . . I will then reflect on my own response to this challenge in respect of my own teaching and investigate what I could have done and what I can do later in my placement to improve learning and teaching for the child. (Selina Webb, unpublished 2008)*

Not all essay titles leave room for customising in this way. 'Analyse how ICT can support creative learning and teaching in the core subjects' is a straightforward instruction. It lends itself to an initial discussion of the issues raised and illustration by example from experience in school.

The conclusion

The generally accepted pattern for a conclusion is that it summarises the main points raised in the essay. The danger with this is that it if the conclusion does not say or reveal anything new from the accumulation of the insights already discussed it will be superfluous. In the following example in response to the instruction, 'With specific reference to a particular literacy lesson which you have taught, identify and discuss two strengths and two growth points', the student successfully makes one new, more general point not explicitly stated in the essay itself. In the essay they had described situations that were leading towards this broader point, such as, 'My lesson did not follow the typical Literacy Hour structure; however I do not feel that for this task it was necessary. I still incorporated many objectives from the (Literacy Strategy) . . .'. However, they held back from drawing the main conclusion which is as follows:

> *The National Literacy Strategy (NLS) is only recommended. It is a guide to how we the teachers can provide our children with the opportunity to reach the required targets set by the National Curriculum. It will not always be appropriate to follow exactly the structure of the Literacy Hour. It is an excellent starting point, however, and truly has, in my opinion '. . . substantially raised literacy standards among primary school children by encouraging teachers to reach reading and writing in ways which have not been widely used in England' (Beard, 2000, p. 245). It is a matter of exercising our own discretion to decide the techniques that will aid the children most successfully to reach their full potential. (Lauren Smith, unpublished 2004)*

Practical task

Read the following extracts from the essay, 'Creating and maintaining a safe learning environment'. In the light of the quoted introduction, consider what the content of the conclusion might be.

> *I taught a lesson on adverbs . . . that turned out to be the most exciting and engaging lesson I'd taught due to the many opportunities I gave to the children to participate and the encouragement and praise I gave them. During the lesson I didn't have to discipline a single child once. . .In the safe environment that had been created the children realised that they could get praise and attention by producing good behaviour and contributing to the lesson in a meaningful way. (Victoria Collier, unpublished 2007)*

Now compare your thoughts with those of the student in question by finding their conclusion at the end of this chapter. What you will find there is a direct logical line connecting the introduction, the content and the conclusion.

Structuring the main content of the essay

Your university programme is vocational and therefore is primarily concerned with developing practice. The purpose of academic study in relation to this practice is to encourage a reflective and informed approach. The brief of an essay will commonly expect any theoretical idea to be illustrated by examples from your own experience. If this is done appropriately (i.e. it illustrates the theoretical point fully, not vaguely or in part), it will demonstrate that you are operating at a reflective level. In some forms of writing you may be expected to discuss a theoretical point, back it with reference to relevant literature and then illustrate it with reference to your own experience. Here a student first writes theoretically about creativity and then gives an example of her own experience:

> *The Plowden Report said over forty years ago: 'At the heart of the educational process lies the child.' If the child is truly to be central, creativity and originality must be paramount, otherwise the child is the passive recipient of information . . .*
>
> *Immediately on entering the area of my first placement school it was obvious that there is encouragement of learning through play . . . There is an area on the corridor outside the classrooms where books and other activities linked to current topics can be found. (Christine Everett, unpublished 2008)*

These would be reversed in another form of essay in which a student is being encouraged to develop her own ideas and theories first. The example could be analysed as an example of a school environment that encouraged active and independent learning by children. Only then would the writer refer to other authorities in the literature that she had been reading.

Clerical tasks of editing and checking

You will not need reminding that the essay must be read through and checked for minor errors, fluency and sense. Unfortunately, tutors will write too often in an essay report that there are spelling and grammatical errors and that it would benefit from careful and critical reading. An artist will sometimes spend a period of time up close to the canvas working on detail. It is only when he or she stands back that it is clear that the colour balance has been upset or the angle of the nose on a portrait is wrong because the part could not be assessed in relation to the whole canvas when viewed close up. The same is true for writing. One read-through of an essay from beginning to end is necessary to judge whether the argument really does hold together. Also take care with paragraphing, to ensure that each paragraph has a central theme which is clear from the beginning.

Then there should be attention to the clerical tasks. After a spell check from the computer, another read-through will finally show up spellings that will not have been caught by the electronics (e.g. form/from).

Only after these important checks is the piece ready to be bundled into a folder and submitted.

Summary of key points

When you quote your own journal or school file in an essay, try to add a critically analytical element to it by, for instance, checking your opinions against your more recent thinking.

Check that you are being reflective by using the three aspects of reflectivity defined by Boud et al.:

1   *returning to experience;*

2   *attending to feelings;*

3   *evaluating experience.*

You may want to evaluate your level of reflectivity against the four grades created by Kember et al.:

1   *habitual action;*

2   *understanding;*

3   *reflection;*

4   *critical reflection.*

Make sure your essay introduction lets the reader know what the main themes of your writing are.

Reserve an interesting feature or general point for the conclusion. This may well be what you have learned from the experience of writing, which will have impact on your teaching in the future.

Make sure you allow time for the clerical tasks of editing and checking. Lack of care makes your work appear unprofessional.

The conclusion as written by Victoria Collier in the Practical Task about the content of an essay conclusion.

While at first I believed creating and maintaining a safe learning environment was about disciplining children to produce good behaviour, I now see there are many preventative steps that come prior to this that are concerned with the environment the children are in. Creating a positive working environment as described in this paper can reduce the likelihood of bad behaviour, and therefore reduce the need for discipline.

References and further reading

Beard, R. (2000) *Developing writing 3–13*. London Hodder and Stoughton.

Beveridge, A.N. (1997) Teaching your students to think reflectively: the case for reflective journals. *Teaching in Higher Education*, 2(1). pp. 33–43

Boud, D. Keogh, R. and Walker, D. (1985) *Reflection: turning experience into learning*. London: Kogan.

Cheeseman, P.L. and Watts, P.E. (1985) *Positive behaviour management: a manual for teachers*. London, Croom Helm.

Dewey, J. (1933) *How we think*. New York: D.C. Heath.

DfES (1999) *All our futures: creativity, culture and education*. London: HMSO.

DfES Central Advisory Council for Education (1967) *Children and their primary schools* ('The Plowden Report'). London: HMSO.

Kember, D., McKay, J., Sinclair, K. and Kam Yuet Wong, F. (August 2008) A four category scheme for coding and assessing the level of reflection in written work. *Assessment and Evaluation in Higher Education*, 33(4): pp. 369–379.

Index